Heartfelt Whispers

Poornacharanya Rajaguru

BookLeaf Publishing

India | USA | UK

Made with ❤ on the BookLeaf Publishing Platform
www.bookleafpub.in
www.bookleafpub.com

Dedication

*To every soul feeling lonely in the fight against its own
battles*

Preface

"And miles to before I sleep" has always been a guiding star in my life, a reminder that the journey is far from over. Growing up, I often found it difficult to navigate the landscape of my emotions. It was only when I embarked on the path of self-love that I discovered the quiet, powerful solace of writing.

This book is a testament to that journey- a collection of poems that became my refuge, my way of healing, and my means of moving forward. Through these words, I found peace, and I hope that within them, you might find a glimmer of the same.

Acknowledgements

*To my husband who is kind and has helped me
become a better human being.
To my parents who have worked hard to make my
dreams come true.
To my supportive family and loving friends.*

Rainy Day

On bright days, I'm clear as the sky,
Determined, with goals set high.

But when doubts come, I'm a cloudy gray,
Wondering if I'll find my way.

Will I be fine? Will I stay clear?
Like clouds that hang, when rain's not near.

I wish for strength, like skies that pour,
Holding back, then giving more.

I wish to shine, like the sun so bright,
Doing what I want in its light.

Not to hide behind clouds in gray,
But to come out and shine each day.

Winter's Reflections

The city was silent in the winter,
And so was my heart each time I gazed out the window.

The city was unpredictable with its weather,
And so was my heart each time I faced a decision in my life.

The city rattled with the winter storm,
And so did my heart each time I let someone new into my life.

The city grew quieter as the snow fell,
And my heart grew still as I watched the world outside.

The city could change from sunny to cloudy in an instant,
Just as my heart could waver between hope and doubt.

The city felt the chill of the storm,
And my heart felt the same cold when I welcomed someone new, unsure of what they'd bring.

Yet, the city always found a way to endure the winter,
And my heart, too, learned to weather its own storms.

With every snowflake, the city remained resilient,
And with every heartbeat, I found strength to keep
going.

The city and my heart, both silent and stormy,
Both unpredictable and strong,
Both finding their way through the winter,
Both looking ahead to spring.

Seeking Calm Amidst Waters

Under the calm sky's embrace,
I long for a tranquil space,
Emotions stir, like winds that plea,
Seeking stillness, like the sea.

May my heart be a tranquil lake,
Rippling gently, solace to make,
Not roaring waves that wildly soar,
But steady waters at the core.

As winds and currents hold their sway,
I'll anchor firm, come what may,
In deep calm depths, strength does lie,
Tranquility found, as storms pass by.

When life's tempests start to brew,
I'll channel skies of peaceful blue,
with steady grace, my soul shall be,
A quiet lake, not a raging sea.

Echoes From Within

There is grief in distance from the past,
Guilt in staying away from its harm.
Perspective lost when the ground shakes,
Fear in knowing you were unprotected.

Conflict between shielding yourself,
And the pain of leaving home behind.
Tired from constant suffering,
Pushing to live in the now.

Triggers from old wounds in new ties,
Judgement from yourself and others.
No one knows how to handle it,
No one knows right from wrong.

Self-hate when others smile through pain,
Low esteem when you can't bear yours.
Trust lost in those meant to love,
Suffering lingers, always present.

Staying positive feels so hard,
Dreams and hopes seem far away.
What's the point of chasing peace,
When it feels so out of reach?

Everything But Me

The sky was clear,
Everything felt right, except me.
The lake was calm,
Everything was still, except me.

The world seemed perfect,
Everything was in place, except me.
The birds were singing,
Their songs were happy, but I was not.

The flowers bloomed,
Their colors were bright, but I felt dull.
The sun was shining,
Its warmth was comforting, but I felt cold.

The breeze was gentle,
It brought peace to all, except me.
The stars were sparkling,
They lit up the night, but I felt dark.

The moon was glowing,
Its light was soothing, but I felt lost.
The earth was turning,
It carried on, while I stood still.

What If

What if we were never meant to be home?
What if we accepted each other
because we were too tired to start anew?
What if we made each other home
out of fear of being alone?

What if we stayed together,
not ready to be vulnerable with someone new?
What if we convinced ourselves we were destined,
having lost our one true love?

What if we chose each other
as the safe option, not the right place?
What if we were never meant to be home?
What if we had never met?
What then?

What Should I Do

What should I do when the hands that should shield me from the cruelties around the world is the one causing harm?

What should I do when they don't respect me as a human even though deep down I know you are a way better human being than them?

What should I do everyone around me wants have a free will but they keep snatching mine every opportunity they get ?

What should I do everyone around me wants to be the savior when I actually need saving from myself ?

What should I do ? It's overwhelming. It's so painful that the relief of ripping my heart out and dying this instant feels peaceful.

What should I do when everyone expects me to take care of their dignity when everyone stole mine ?

Balancing The Heart

Learning to stop overcompensating feels guilty,
Like I'm neglecting those I care about,
Yet in this newfound restraint,
I begin to understand the roots of true happiness,
No longer burdened by the weight of doing too much.

Learning to stop overcompensating feels selfish,
As if I'm putting myself above others' needs,
But in this space, I start to see things more clearly,
Recognizing the value of balance,
And how it lets me appreciate life in a different light.

Learning to stop overcompensating means facing my
fears,
The worry that I am not enough,
Yet it brings a quiet strength,
A deeper connection to myself,
Allowing me to offer my best to the world without losing
who I am.

Learning to stop overcompensating clears my vision,
Helping me see people and situations as they truly are,
No longer clouded by the fog of doing too much,
I find clarity and peace,

And the courage to live a life that's balanced and
fulfilled.

Reclaiming My Fight

I wanted honesty, clarity,
You gave me manipulation, doubt.
I wanted hopes, dreams,
You handed me anxiety, confusion.
I sought quiet, happiness,
You delivered chaos, misery.

I needed love, protection,
You offered self-hate, loneliness.
I craved freedom of expression,
You gave me independence.
I desired support, encouragement,
You left me to fend for myself.

I wanted you to want me,
You made me realize I am your biggest failure.
I sought protection from you,
You still protect yourself.
I longed for unconditional love,
You laid your expectations upon me.

I searched for quiet within myself,
You demanded chaos.
I wished to be fine,

You wanted extraordinary.
For when I asked for the ordinary,
You didn't give the bare minimum.

I am strong,
You think I'm in over my head.
I am loved,
You feel disconnected.
I am free,
You want me caged.

I aspire to fly high,
You try to anchor me.
For I am no longer a home bird,
I am a migrant now.
I am fighting for my life,
I will not fight you.

For I no longer see myself as a fighter,
Because I am an optimist.

Balancing The Unseen

Ignorant in love,
Careless with self-love,
Lost in the rush of emotions,
Forgetting what it means to care for oneself.

Careful in love,
Dedicated to self-love,
Learning to balance the two,
Yet feeling the weight of every choice made.

Fueled by rage,
Running on fear,
Living with uncertainty,
Each step forward feeling like a leap into the unknown.

But still, we find the courage to live,
To keep moving forward,
Even when the path is unclear,
Such is today's reality,
Where love, self, and career collide,
And we struggle to find where we belong.

We try to be everything at once,
A lover, a fighter, a dreamer,

But in the chaos, we must remember,
That it's okay to pause, to breathe, to be unsure,
Because we are all just trying to make it through,
In a world that never stops demanding more.

Focus And Balance

Focus on one thing makes the rest blurry,
Finding peace within makes worries fade away.

Focus on one thing, and all else turns foggy,
Finding home away makes you feel lonely.

Focus on one thing, and the rest is left behind,
Finding true purpose can leave you tired.

Focus on one thing, and you may become blind,
Finding your priorities makes you stronger.

Focus on one thing, and everything seems tough,
Finding perspective makes you better.

From Then To Now

Back then,
Dance taught me discipline,
Third language classes, hard work,
Homework taught me routine,
Being the school topper gave me motivation,
Competitions gave me enthusiasm.

As a kid, I dreamed big,
As a child, I hoped big,
As a teenager, I was open to new things.

Now,
Dance reels make me envious,
People speaking multiple languages make me insecure,
Work makes me tired,
New beginnings make me anxious.

As an adult, I am scared,
As I grow older, I'm not open to change,
As a grown-up, I'm not okay with starting something
new.

Somewhere between then and now, I changed,
From an overachiever to just getting through the day, I

am skeptical,
Somewhere growing up, I lost myself.

Is it good or bad? I don't know,
Will I be the same? I have no answer,
Do I want more? Yes,
Am I content with what I have? Yes.

Where does my life go next? I don't know,
What do I know? Everything will be fine.

The world Between Pages

In books, I find a sense of home,
A place where I can relate,
A comfort I often miss in the world,
A bond that doesn't hesitate.

Books give me a sense of promise,
A hope I struggle to create,
They show me dreams worth dreaming,
While life demands I run, not wait.

Reading gives me hope and strength,
That I am not alone,
A space to let my mind roam free,
To imagine, to grow, to own.

Books teach me to love this life,
With all its twists and turns,
They make me who I am today,
In every page, my spirit burns.

F1 And Life

In Formula 1, a tale is told,
Of triumph and defeat, bold and cold.
One team basks in victory's glow,
While another ponders what went low.

Teammates, side by side they race,
Yet one shines bright in the embrace,
Of fame and glory, leaving the other behind,
Though both gave their all, equally kind.

Life mirrors this, unfair sometimes,
Where one's success, another's climbs.
Yet in the end, we must find peace,
Celebrate the winner, from envy, release.

For life, like F1, tests our grit,
To accept defeat, but never quit.
To focus on the future, strive for more,
And in the journey, find what we're living

Marathon Of Choices

Now, my life stands at an impasse.

Searching for the missing piece,
I ran towards the unknown as a child.

Fearing the unknown and muffling my heart,
I ran towards a familiar devil.

Dreading the prospect of becoming a known monster,
I ran towards unfamiliar mistakes.

Terrified of losing to my errors,
I ran towards the unknown.

Weary from running towards the unknown,
I sought something new.

Haunted by the fear of becoming a known monster,
I constantly chased after perplexity.

Running turned into a marathon;
I never knew when to give up.

After enduring countless hardships to reach the finish

line,
My life has come to an impasse.

With so many goals to achieve,
And many alliances to tend to,
Should I reminisce about this marathon for a comforting
destiny,
Or continue running marathons for a varied existence?

The Balance Within

You're meant to have your own voice,
But not in ways that wound others.

You're meant to be independent,
But not in ways that bruise their pride.

You're allowed to shed your tears,
But with them, not to them, nor at them.

You're meant to love without bounds,
But can't expect the same in return.

Is it wrong? Yes and no.
Is it right? No and yes.
We each have our own thresholds,
And the real struggle lies
In choosing who pays the price—
Them, or you.

Sunshine And Mermaid

He was her sunshine, she was his mermaid.

He touched her with his light, urging her to swim higher.

She crossed the sea, offering him a shoulder to call home.

She found colors in his warm saffron light.

He found peace in her hope-filled eyes.

He was her sunshine, she was his mermaid.

Together they understood love, life, and survival.

Definition Of Love

Love is beyond definition,
A dance of space and closeness,
Silence shared, or a warm embrace,
Responding to what they need.

It's standing firm for what matters,
Yet yielding when the bond holds worth,
A balance of independence,
And unyielding affection.

Loving others deeply,
While finding love for yourself,
Amidst the shadows within,
Accepting pain, and moving on.

Love is selfish kindness,
Selfless romance intertwined,
Unconditional care,
With moments of seeking clarity.

No questions asked,
Yet questions asked when needed,
Love is all things at once,
A blend of strength and courage.

To love without ego,
Without fear or need to be right,
Accepting the short straw,
Love is everything, all at once.

Love Is Love

Love is not grand gestures,
 It's finding joy in small treasures.
It's accepting with all your heart,
Even when you have very little part.

Love is in the journey, not the end,
Admitting mistakes, striving to mend.
It's knowing no one's flawless,
Choosing to stay during life's stress.

Love is knowing when to release,
For their well-being, finding peace.
It's also learning to protect your heart,
Taking it slow, one step at a start.

Love is all these things, you see,
A journey of growth and empathy

To The Girl Who Survived It All

To the girl who smiles through the chaos around,
To the girl who stands tall, though her heart's been
unbound,
To the girl who endures, never tired of the fight,
To the girl who seeks the dawn, even in the darkest
night.

To the girl who cries, then rises once more,
To the girl who gives all, though her path is unsure,
To the girl who takes words with a smile and grace,
Yet seeks growth and love, in every space.

To the girl with fire but never with hate,
To the girl who battles, hoping truth finds its state,
To the girl who loves deeply, never letting go,
To the girl who seeks light wherever she roams.

Your bravery and hope are a beacon so bright,
Never let anyone dim your inner light.
For you seek positivity, even when life is tough,
Be brave, be unstoppable, you are enough.

Journey To Thy Unseen Self

Neither here nor there,
Where am I?
Neither here nor there,
Whose am I?
Neither here nor there,
I am my own.

The deep secrets of the heart,
Hidden by the universe,
As I search, I realize,
My identity lies within me.

In search of a destination,
I wander in oblivion,
On illuminated paths, I find myself,
Or even in darkness, I recognize myself.

In the waves of life,
I shall ride each wave,
Embracing moments of joy,
And enfolding sorrows in my smile.

Neither here, nor there,
It's a new journey,

Connecting with myself, finding clarity,
Embracing every challenge,
 Discovering myself on new paths